T0095438

The Element of
FOCUS

The Element of
FOCUS

A STRATEGIC APPROACH TO ACHIEVING YOUR GOALS

Casey "OZ" Osborne

THE ELEMENT OF FOCUS
A Strategic Approach to Achieving Your Goals

iUniverse books may be ordered through booksellers or by contacting:

iUniverse
1663 Liberty Drive
Bloomington, IN 47403
www.iuniverse.com
1-800-Authors (1-800-288-4677)

Because of the dynamic nature of the Internet, any web addresses or links contained in this book may have changed since publication and may no longer be valid. The views expressed in this work are solely those of the author and do not necessarily reflect the views of the publisher, and the publisher hereby disclaims any responsibility for them.

Any people depicted in stock imagery provided by Thinkstock are models, and such images are being used for illustrative purposes only. Certain stock imagery © Thinkstock.

ISBN: 978-1-4917-7404-5 (sc)
ISBN: 978-1-4917-7403-8 (e)

Library of Congress Control Number: 2015914114

Print information available on the last page.

iUniverse rev. date: 09/24/2015

CONTENTS

PREFACE

When I first decided to write this book, I had just a series of personal notes to myself—no more than a collection of thoughts, ideas, and suggestions that has helped me to get past my own stumbling blocks in life. As the number of thoughts and ideas grew exponentially, I came to the conclusion that what I was beginning to put down on paper was not just something that I should reflect upon when I felt stagnant in my own forward progression, but it was something that should be shared with others. Then I thought, *What if there are hundreds or thousands of people out there with unlimited potential to succeed at whatever they desire to achieve but simply cannot get past the pitfalls and distractions in life that hinder us all? Wouldn't it be nice to have a basic point of reference to help us get back on track and keep moving forward?*

So with the simple premise of identifying the things that hold us back and creating ways to eliminate or avoid them, I wrote this book for you, me, and us—all of us. I hope you enjoy it, and I hope it helps you in reaching all your goals, whatever they may be.

Chapter 1

THE MEANING AND VALUE OF FOCUS

For the purpose of this book, the definition of *focus* is to concentrate one's attention in a positive direction without straying from the intended path. As simple as this may sound, millions of people struggle every day to do just that. As someone who has encountered a lack of focus in my endeavors to make progress in my life and help the people around me move forward in a positive direction, I understand this concept as well as, if not better than, anyone. In 90 percent of all cases known to man, failure to achieve a specific goal or to complete a particular task can be attributed to the lack of, loss of, or inability to focus on the goal or task at hand. It is usually only after repetitive failure and disappointment that we learn the value of gaining and maintaining focus.

The purpose of this book is to identify the obstacles that get in the way of us pursuing what makes us happy, eliminate or avoid those things, find ways to stay focused on our paths all the way to the end, and see our dreams to fruition.

There are many different schools of thought when it comes to this topic. Most logic-minded people tend to share my view on the subject, taking the stance that things like luck, fate, and destiny either do not exist or do not have any bearing on our success or failure in life. During my time as a military weapons instructor, I told my students that those things are just excuses or crutches we lean on when things don't go as planned and that we create our own destinies by making conscious decisions to move forward in a particular direction and not allowing anything or anyone to convince us that it cannot be done.

My mother told me something when I was twelve that had stuck with me my whole life, and to her amazement I recently quoted it back to her verbatim at age thirty-six. She said, "Freedom is a state of mind, and no one controls a mind better than he who has one." The term *freedom* in her statement refers to mental or emotional freedom. This type of freedom allows us to eliminate or avoid negative factors that may become stumbling blocks on the road to personal success or achievement.

I like to think that the reason I've been successful at certain things I wasn't sure I could accomplish is because I don't place limits on myself. That is, I don't allow people or other situations to dictate what my abilities are. Sometimes I have found it useful to take a slightly different approach to tackling certain tasks. At times I like to point myself in the direction I want to go and simply affirm to myself that no obstacle I may encounter is stronger than my will to succeed at my selected task. By *obstacle* I mean people, events, situations, negative feelings and emotions, or anything that would prevent me from hitting my mark. It's almost like using the Jedi mind trick on yourself; if you don't acknowledge any limits on what you can achieve or accomplish, those limits don't exist and therefore cannot affect your progress or success. Sound a little crazy? It's a simple formula that has worked for me over the last twenty-two years; I'm almost positive that you and the people close to you can benefit from it also.

So far I have given a pretty specific definition of exactly what focus is as it pertains to this book, but how do you assign a value to focus? Well, that's different for everyone and cannot be determined by one for all. I will tell you, however, that a good way to assess the value of focus is to first determine the value of the goal you are trying to reach. Put simply, the value placed on your level of focus should be equal to or greater than the level of importance placed on your personal goals and achievements. If something is extremely important to you, be extremely committed to avoiding the obstacles mentioned earlier in an effort to reach your desired outcome. If the value placed on your end product does not exceed that of the other facets of your life, the whole process of trying to reach your goal is an exercise in futility.

Obviously, I'm not suggesting that we abandon all our personal responsibilities (kids, spouses, family members, etc.) in pursuit of our own selfish ambitions. However, the only way to take a serious approach to reaching personal and professional goals is to be 100 percent committed to becoming a finisher.

Many of us have mastered the art of starting important and sometimes life-altering projects. In fact, most of us have even evolved into highly skilled multitaskers. But finishers are a rare and unique breed. They have an uncanny knack for not only spearheading great undertakings but also consistently implementing the all-important step of follow-through. What separates finishers from the rest of us is the fact that they religiously practice the Three Ps.

You may be thinking, *Great, more cryptic rambling!* But stick with me, and I'll explain. The Three Ps are patience, persistence, and perseverance. *Patience* is the most basic building block of establishing and maintaining focus. The reason for this is that nothing worthwhile comes easily or quickly. So without a substantial amount of patience, you will not stick around long enough to see your dreams realized. *Persistence* is key to completing any task, because if everyone who ever set out to do something gave up at the first sign of rejection or adversity, we would have been deprived of many social, cultural, and technological advances that have made our everyday lives simpler and less taxing. *Perseverance* and patience tend to go hand in hand. Patient people realize that great achievements do not happen overnight; people with perseverance possess a high level of stick-to-itiveness that won't allow them to quit when things become difficult. A combination of all these attributes in large quantities is the primary composition of a true finisher.

Chapter 2

TYPES OF DISTRACTIONS

It's such a simple idea to pick a goal and just stay the course, but we Americans find it extremely difficult sometimes to stay focused long enough to finish anything we start. This could be due to the almost limitless number of distractions we have—TV, video games, malls, restaurants, social events, sporting events, friends, boyfriends/girlfriends, cell phones, and the Internet. Or it could be the never-ending albeit unavoidable list of distractions that are a natural part of life—coworkers, spouses, children, work, and school, as well as financial, spiritual, and health issues.

Our aim should be to break these distractions down into two basic categories—controlled distractions and uncontrolled distractions—followed by two subcategories. Controlled distractions are in the first list above, and we subject ourselves to them out of boredom, habit, routine, emotions, or peer pressure. Uncontrolled distractions are the items in the second list above. These are the things we simply cannot push aside, due to the personal or professional importance they hold.

The two subcategories are necessary distractions and unnecessary distractions. These terms are interchangeable beneath the two main categories, depending on the nature of the situation at hand and what level of personal importance they hold for you. For example, social events and significant others are controlled distractions. But for most emotionally well-adjusted people, these are also necessary distractions because without them we would be focused but extremely detached from the rest of society. Your success is contingent on the importance of attaining your goals balanced against the importance and types of distractions you encounter frequently.

So, how do you maintain a firm grasp on your focus without becoming a socially dysfunctional outcast? The answer is simple, but much easier said than done. In an attempt to stay focused without neglecting the people and things that are important to you, you must strive daily to separate your distractions into the correct categories and strike a healthy balance between the two.

As a man who suffers from obsessive-compulsive disorder, combined with a propensity to look at life from an all-or-nothing viewpoint, I've struggled to maintain balance for the entire forty-two years I've been on this planet. So I understand what a huge challenge this can be for some of us. My family and friends have told me on many occasions that I'm always one extreme or the other and that life's gray areas are problematic for me. I've tried hard to grasp the gray areas, or middle ground, in the last few years of my life. My own trials with finding compromise in my decision-making processes motivated me to write this book.

This balance makes it easier for us to choose who and what goes into which category and therefore frees our minds to focus our energy in the areas that will eventually lead to achieving our goals. There will undoubtedly come a time when you find it extremely difficult to find balance in your life. It could be due to a family or personal crisis, a financial situation, or simply the stresses of everyday life. This is when you have to reach into your mental tool bag and pull out the Three Ps. These three basic stepping-stones will help you to get past temporary rough patches. In short, if you apply some of the basic theories and principles contained within these, you can avoid pitfalls that might prevent your success.

Chapter 3

PEOPLE, PLACES, AND THINGS

Let's take a more in-depth look at specific aspects of the distractions mentioned in the previous chapter and identify some constructive ways to deal with them. When it comes to managing distractions, it is imperative to understand what a huge impact *people, places,* and *things* have on your ability to focus. These three distractions make such a difference because they tend to affect your environment, so we'll call these environmental distractions.

Why does your environment matter? Because your objective should be to create an environment that is conducive to achieving your goal, and the easiest way to do this is to eliminate, avoid, or manage all distractions that may prevent that from happening.

The first on our list of environmental distractions is people. Hundreds of people are in most of our lives at any given time—for a few of us, even thousands. In an effort to gain and maintain your focus, you have to learn to avoid negative people, or "haters." Now, just so we're clear (and to keep you from breaking out your Ebonics/Slang Dictionary) a hater is anyone whose opinions, attitudes, or demeanor is negative or clearly against you reaching your goals or making progress. Usually these people lack the focus, ambition, or courage to pursue their own dreams and aspirations. Since misery loves company, haters love nothing more than to see you fail. Do not give them the satisfaction of impeding your progress.

Obviously, haters and other people that do not directly affect your success or failure do not matter, so it is easy to cut them out of your life. But what about family and friends? These people are necessary uncontrolled distractions and cannot simply be pushed aside. This is where things get tricky and require a great deal of tact and consideration.

There will inevitably come a time when your personal pursuits will conflict with your responsibilities to those you love. With children, spouses, and parents, this can be especially difficult to manage without slowing or halting your forward momentum. These are the people who depend on you the most, require the most of your attention, and will most likely be there cheering for you when you reach your goal.

The nature of your relationship and the personality of your loved one will dictate how you choose to deal with the delicate balancing act you face. If your spouse is supportive and fully comprehends the importance of you reaching your selected milestone, not only should he or she understand what you're going through but actually assist you by picking up some of the slack when it comes to spending time with children, parents, etc. However, make sure that you don't alienate your spouse in the interest of your personal pursuits. This is extremely selfish and will ruin your marriage. Your children may have the hardest time with your preoccupation because by nature they want, need, and demand your time (and not always when it's convenient for you). So if there is any sacrifice of your focus, this is where that energy should be directed.

Here are some ways to balance your commitment to your children with your commitment to yourself: Include them in what you do, and praise them for allowing you to concentrate. Giving children ownership in a process makes them feel included and lets them know they are still important to you. Acknowledging the role they play in your success gives them a sense of pride, develops a good work ethic in them, and may inspire them to become finishers as they grow older. Remember that children are a blessing from God and are major achievements themselves, so don't focus on one achievement while neglecting another. Cherish every moment you have with your children because one day they will grow up and move on with their own lives. How frequently they come home for visits later may depend on how important you make them feel now. Obviously, there are exceptions, but as a rule, children tend to be loyal to parents that put them first.

So far we've dealt with spouses, parents, and children, but friends are a completely different category. Some friends are so close that they are considered and even treated like family. Best friends are the most difficult to manage when it comes to dividing your time between them and what you are attempting to accomplish. These are friends who, because of the nature of your relationship, assume and sometimes expect that any free time you have that is not dedicated to your immediate family should belong to them. Basically, best friends are interdependent social beings who crave your attention. Again, you do not want to disregard your best friend, because this is someone who will inevitably make up your cheering section later on.

With your friends, stress the importance of the major milestone you are about to cross and that you need their support and understanding to reach your goal. Hopefully they will take this as an opportunity to contribute to your success, appreciate the fact that they are important to you, and be proud that you are taking positive steps to better yourself as a human being. If this positive and desirable outcome is not the result, you may have to consider that the person may be going through a personal crisis or may truly be a hater. A best friend will understand the meaning of true friendship and be happy for you, gladly allowing you the time to "do work" and make things happen the way you need them to.

Next on our list of environmental distractions is places. The place where you choose to work on your goals plays a huge role in how effective you are at achieving them. The environment you create for yourself will or will not help you gain and maintain focus. Set yourself up for success by selecting a location that is consistently quiet, very comfortable, and easily accessible.

If you have a family, this can be particularly challenging, especially if you have small children at home. Even if your children are older, they generally are not very quiet, ask a lot of questions, and basically do not comprehend the need for a distraction-free environment when attempting to focus on a task or goal. You may want to create a room or section of your house that is set up for the sole purpose of helping you achieve your goals without completely isolating yourself from the rest of the family.

People without families have a little more creative freedom when it comes to selecting the ideal work location. Not having the added responsibility of "obligatory time sharing" makes it easier to get things done on your own time. Your environmental distractions might not be people or things, but events, excursions, or outings that take you away from your primary task. Examples of this would be drinks with friends, shopping, or ball games. There is no magic trick, tip, or formula for avoiding this type of distraction. This is where willpower, discipline, and supportive friends and family come into play. Again, giving the people closest to you some ownership in the achievement of your goal will make them more apt to support your need to avoid the things that distract you.

Chapter 4

THE IMPORTANCE OF SIMPLICITY

One of the most important factors in personal success is to recognize the value of keeping things simple. This encompasses not only the simplicity of the task at hand but also the approach used to complete that task. Now, just so we're clear, I am not suggesting that every endeavor you embark on should or will be a walk in the park. Instead, I urge you to avoid complicating your journey with anything unnecessary or premature. When I decided to write this book, I found myself overwhelmed with the details. Where do I start? What should the format be? How do I find an editor? How much will it cost? All these concerns were stifling my thought process and even my ability to get started. Because of my obsessive-compulsive disorder, I tend to think four steps ahead.

Fortunately, my intuitive (and awesome) mother, Cynthia, has a knack for reeling me back in and putting things in perspective for me. She told me to relax, to remember that all the details would be worked out later, and to concentrate on getting my thoughts onto paper first. This is just one personal example of how we can complicate things if we get ahead of ourselves. Having a close friend, family member, or significant other to keep you grounded can be a huge asset in keeping things simple. I can attest to this because I have been blessed with a magnificent support system that helps me stay focused. Without my mother, my older brother, Dennis, and my four awesome daughters (Jalyssa, Jayneece, Jaylynn, and Jessinia), I would be lost.

Another way to avoid unnecessary complication is to break your entire goal down into steps. As you do this, you will begin to view every stage of your process as a step closer to the completion of your task. As an instructor in the military, I used a process called lockstepping, which involves approaching a particular objective one instructional block at a time. This allowed students to assimilate one portion of the lesson fully before moving on to the next. The students built on each block of instruction and eventually gained full comprehension of the entire objective. I applied this principle to other aspects of my life and found that it worked the same way. In short, it is more difficult to eat an entire pie in a day than to eat a slice a day for a week.

Until now, we have looked at goal-achieving simplicity from a procedural perspective. Another aspect of keeping things simple is to monitor the *content* of the process—that is, limit the components of what it takes to reach your goal. People who are highly adept at multitasking find this difficult because they are used to dealing with multiple situations at once with ease. It is a highly sought-after trait in employees, especially in this age of "more with less." But when seeking simplicity, it can truly be a hindrance. The key to getting past what seems like monotony to multitaskers is learning to appreciate the ease of the step they are working on and fight the urge to complicate it.

Become a follower of the "if it ain't broke, don't fix it" philosophy. Consider mechanics: the fewer moving parts there are, the lower the odds of things breaking. This attitude can help smooth the transition between steps toward your goal and is probably the most fundamental in keeping you from becoming overwhelmed. Depending on the task at hand, this is easier said than done, but it should definitely be something you work at daily.

Every journey requires a road to get there, and every road has warning signs. Do not confuse keeping things simple with overlooking crucial details or steps. This is a common error, especially for those of us who tend to comprehend most information in a literal sense. Creating a simple checklist and making limited notes can aid in avoiding this pitfall. Do not overanalyze individual steps or the process as a whole. This goes hand in hand with the last warning sign and is a suggestion to maintain balance. People like me, who have analytical minds, tend to look deeply into every aspect of everything.

However, do not allow simplicity to cause you to lose interest. The goal of simplicity is to make things easier; in this case, it's to simplify the individual steps of a process. For some, if tasks are easy to complete, boredom results. Strive to recognize this early, and adjust the level of difficulty—or parts to your machine—to keep your interest.

Consider using the crawl-walk-run approach to arranging your checklist. This may sound like military babble, but stay with me. Try to prioritize the items on your checklist in order of importance and level of difficulty. Once this is done, decide if it will be possible to move between these two categories smoothly, and start with the least stressful step. Successful completion of that first step will feel like a reward and will fuel you to continue with more confidence. As your confidence grows, so will your ability to tackle more difficult tasks. Again, this is similar to lock-stepping and lends itself to perpetual progress.

These are just a few simple techniques to assist in keeping your steps simple and ensuring the eventual achievement of your goals. Every technique does not work for every individual, but the more tools you have to succeed, the better your chances.

Chapter 5

IDENTIFYING YOUR GOALS

Before you set out on a journey to achieve a specific goal or set of goals, it's imperative that you clearly identify what you expect to achieve. Identifying your goals is a crucial part of any progressive process because if you don't get this part right, your path will be wrought with confusion, frustration, and duplication of effort.

I don't know about you, but one thing I despise more than anything when trying to accomplish a task is duplicating work. When I was a child, my grandfather used to tell me, "If you do something right the first time, you won't have to keep doing it over and over again." At the time he was talking about chores around the house, but my grandfather was a very wise man so I clung to his every word. This is just one of many pearls of wisdom given to me by a great man and like many things that sprang from his lips, I applied it to my everyday life. I make frequent reference to my grandfather because, in the absence of my biological father, he provided me with 90 percent of the paternal guidance my life was lacking. The rest I extracted from positive male role models over the last two decades.

Taking the time to clearly and properly identify your goals will give you a clear starting point and save you valuable time later on. Dedicating a reasonable amount of time to this most crucial step will set the foundation for all the hard work that will follow.

The process of identifying your goals may seem simple enough. You might think that all you have to do is make a list of important items and check them off as you go. For achieving the simplest of goals, this approach is more than adequate. But if your overall goal will require a great amount of planning, logistics, and hard work, you will need to use a more systematic blueprint.

First, do backward planning. This process consists of starting at the end result of whatever it is you are trying to achieve and then listing in reverse order what it will take to meet your goal. This may sound abstract, but we do it all the time without realizing it. For example, when you decide to go somewhere, you pick your destination first, then use a map app or your GPS to find out how to get there, right? Your ultimate goal is your destination, and the individual steps taken to achieve that goal are portions of your map.

By using this strategy, you can simplify the process through a logical sequence of events that leads you to where you need to start. Carefully review your steps to ensure that they will help you achieve your overall goal. Once you know the path required to reach your destination, you can simply use the Three Ps to complete one leg of your trip at a time.

This is where the lockstepping process discussed in the previous chapter comes in handy. Having a clearly defined set of minigoals to achieve makes attaining overall success easier. Also, building on the achievement of the previous task will help you to stay motivated and prevent you from feeling overwhelmed. Becoming bogged down or emotionally overtaxed with the details of everything that lies ahead can be detrimental at this early stage in reaching your goal. Some of us tend to get ahead of ourselves by considering our overall goal achievement. For this reason, it is imperative that those who have trouble maintaining perspective take each phase one step at a time. Remember: crawl, walk, run.

It may be easy for you to assume that the steps leading to your end result are concrete and unchangeable. This is untrue, but any modifications should be approached with caution. (Multitaskers, beware). If you are working on one of your steps and you find that it needs to be modified or is unnecessary, change or eliminate that step. My warning here is simple: consider the effects of that action on your overall goal, and use a logic-based process to decide whether such a change is warranted.

It is important to stay flexible during this process, but unnecessary changes, additions, or deletions to your road map will only complicate your journey and clutter your "mental desk"—that is, the collection of thoughts and ideas that are relevant to the task at hand. Making a conscious effort to keep our thoughts clear gives us the mental and emotional freedom required for personal success. An uncluttered mental desk provides a blank canvas on which the paint brushes of creativity can run amok! I realize that I use an exorbitant amount of metaphors and anecdotal references throughout this whole book, but I assure you they serve a purpose, because you are still reading LOL!

Whether your ultimate goal is one you plan to duplicate in the future or not, it may be a good idea to document the steps that led to your success. This will serve two purposes: One, it will be a record of multiple accomplishments, as your minigoals will be included on the list. Maintaining a tangible memento of your achievements will promote a sense of pride and possibly inspire you to reach for the next achievement. Two, having a previously documented "road map" will aid in future achievement of the same or a similar goal. If you keep your printout from a map app, your next trip to the same destination will be easier.

If this documentation contains critical business secrets or trademark processes, safeguard it as necessary. If blueprints, manuscripts, original drafts of written works, and written steps of a process fall into the wrong hands, it can be devastating to your efforts. Would-be haters and other people with negative motives would love to take advantage of all your hard work. So protect these items with your life, and view them from time to time.

Ultimately, identifying your goals will simplify the process of achieving success at whatever you set out to do. Having a systematic way of doing this will help you to avoid frustration, mistakes, and duplications, all of which are counterproductive in terms of your achievements.

Chapter 6

RECOGNIZING YOUR OWN POTENTIAL

No matter how humble we may be, as human beings we have an inherent ability to know what our strengths and weaknesses are. This trait is pivotal in the pursuit of any goal or achievement because it is crucial to be able to identify what you are good at and to be able to capitalize on the qualities that will aid in your success. It is equally (if not more) important to have the ability to recognize the attributes that you simply do not possess. Identifying these two things early in your quest will prove beneficial in the long run. Recognizing your potential will help to prevent potential pitfalls on the road to goal achievement.

Knowing where you excel and fall short will also give you an opportunity to find suitable workarounds in the areas that are not your strong suit. In the preplanning phase of your ultimate outcome, make a list of your minigoals. Next, make a list of your qualities, traits, or attributes that directly contribute to the achievement of those goals. I call this process "goal and ability matching." It is relatively simple and will give you an opportunity to see where you may need outside help to continue your forward progression.

It is extremely important to be completely honest with yourself when matching your goals with your abilities.

There is absolutely no room for ego, false bravado, or narcissism in this process. If you are not accurate in identifying your strengths and weaknesses, the truth will certainly come out later and may cause stress, anxiety, and feelings of failure. All these emotions are negative and may stifle your progress.

Just as it is important to be honest about what you are capable of, do not overlook your proficiency at certain tasks. A positive mental attitude and self-confidence are critical ingredients of your success. Most of us know that it is difficult to believe in people who do not believe in themselves. With that in mind, you must continuously excel where you can and have the wisdom and humility to seek assistance from competent sources when necessary.

When it becomes necessary to outsource, try to find subject-matter experts (SMEs) to help you make your finished product the best it can be. I consider myself a jack-of-all-trades and a master of none. I know a little bit about everything and a lot about nothing. While this has made me a well-rounded member of society and granted me the ability to hold conversations in almost any circle, it does not lend itself to specificity. Someone with a similar skill set is not the person I want assisting me in a goal-specific task.

Poll the people around you (coworkers, family members, local professionals) to find specialists whose expertise satisfies your needs in a particular area. This search can sometimes be easier if you ask older or more seasoned individuals that are "in the know." These people will usually have a breadth of experience (personal and professional), and they will have already experienced pitfalls through trial and error and may have valuable information to help you avoid the same fate. Most older people are an endless fountain of knowledge and wisdom not to be underestimated.

Earlier we spoke about goal and ability matching to aid in knowing when to ask for help. Also, keep in mind that just because you don't know something doesn't mean that you cannot learn what you need to know on your own. I am a huge fan of the "For Dummies" series of books and the DIY Network. There are countless other sources of information dedicated to teaching you how to do almost anything you can imagine. In fact, most libraries and bookstores have a whole section devoted to the avid do-it-yourselfer.

Some of us are natural learners who have the innate ability to read something, practice it, and become proficient at it in a short time. But some of us need a lot of repetition to become experts, taking a substantial amount of time to master something. Depending on your comprehension abilities and the date you expect to meet your goal, this may or may not be the best solution for you. Do not do everything yourself if it will make you break your own timeline. But do strengthen your knowledge base in the long run. Once you match your goals and abilities, and identify items that require you to outsource, you can proceed with a well-laid-out plan of attack.

In certain cases, you may not be the person actually doing the work that needs to be done. You may be a facilitator or manager of a particular project. One of the key components of being a good leader is being able to put the right people in the right positions to accomplish the overall mission. In these types of situations, all the aforementioned steps are just as critical for goal achievement. The only difference is that instead of performing the tasks yourself, you direct the actions of your subordinates. The trick to this is to be clear and concise when giving instructions and to find ways to set your people up for success.

Make it a point to find workers that function well together and feed off one another's ideas and enthusiasm. Creating small teams like this will create cohesiveness and give team members a sense of ownership. Ultimately, you want the people who are doing the work to feel like they have as much invested in the project as you do. Equally as important as knowing your people's respective talents is being the type of leader that identifies potential problems early and finds viable solutions quickly. The last thing you want is for progress to come to a halt because your team is trying to resolve an issue that the boss should be dealing with.

Your mission should be to think four steps ahead of where your workers are and rectify problems before they become problems. If you are a project manager, keep your hands in every aspect of an operation without micromanaging the process itself. This will allow you to smooth bumps in the road before your workers get to one. Your team will never know there was an issue, but only that you supported them in their every endeavor to succeed. Being a facilitator is one of the most important functions of being a good leader, and it puts workers in a state of mind that is conducive to high-quality work.

This philosophy is not limited to eliminating obstacles to project completion. An effective manager must be intuitive enough to recognize any problems (personal or professional) that team members may encounter. A propensity to assist workers in solving problems of any nature is key to maintaining the focus of the group as a whole and ultimately will aid in project completion. If they feel like you care about their well-being and are willing to take care of their needs, they will be happy and subsequently more productive. Knowing your own potential or the potential of those working with or for you is the foundation for a smooth flow of events toward goal achievement. The process of identifying strengths and weaknesses in yourself and those working with you on a particular project can be full of challenges, but it will pay off in the form of achieving the specified goal.

Chapter 7

THE ELEMENTS OF PRACTICAL PLANNING

When you are deciding to accomplish a specific goal, the planning phase can set the tone for the entire project. Any plan that lacks structure and a systematic sequence of events can cost you valuable time that could be used in a more productive manner. For this reason, it is important to establish a set of standards or rules that will simplify the planning process. In the interest of avoiding time-robbing exercises in futility, I have developed a simple set of guidelines to make this process less painful: the elements of practical planning. They are specificity, accuracy, consistency, and follow-through.

Specificity refers to steps or procedures within your planning process that are specific to the goal at hand. Throwing out random ideas, or spitballing as it is sometimes called, is an unproductive and unprofessional way to develop a comprehensive plan. Random ideas that are not specific to the overall goal will confuse those involved in the planning process and detract from your focus, which should always be on achieving your goal.

Brainstorming, on the other hand, often confused with "spitballing," is much more conducive to effective planning. Brainstorming is generating creative ideas spontaneously, usually for problem solving, and especially in an intensive group activity that does not allow time for reflection. By definition, brainstorming is a method of constructing ideas that will aid in building a solid plan that is specific to the achievement of your desired outcome. While the element of specificity is important to the planning process, I caution you not to be so rigid in your planning that you do not leave room for flexibility (which we will cover in the next chapter).

Accuracy is basically ensuring that the information, facts, and data associated with your project are true, correct, and come from reputable sources. I cannot begin to express how important this element is while developing your plan. Everything you do, from the preplanning phase to project completion, is contingent on the accuracy of the information used to complete your task. Not only can inaccurate information cause you to make mistakes in the execution of your plan, but it also can seriously damage your credibility with the intended benefactors of your completed project. A lack of accuracy can also make you appear incompetent to partners, business associates, and fellow team members.

The use of a subject-matter expert or task-specific reference may be highly useful at this point, especially if a portion of your planning process requires certain facts, statistics, and detailed information. Thorough research and fact finding can help you to avoid duplication of effort and unnecessary pitfalls. Though it can be time consuming, tedious, and sometimes frustrating, the long-term benefits outweigh the short-term aggravation. Like Granddaddy said, "Do it right the first time and you won't have to keep doing it over and over." Taking time to ensure that you have your facts right and that you know what you are talking about will not only inspire self-confidence but also quell doubts in the minds of those you are working with.

Our third element of practical planning is *consistency*, a concept that most people find difficult to master. The textbook definition of consistency is conformity with previous attitudes, behavior, practice, etc.—basically, doing something the same way each time you do it. Why is this is important? First, because it forces you to become more proficient by virtue of repetition. Also, if your end result is one that you plan on repeating, you will need to do everything the same way in order to achieve the same result.

Consistency also comes into play when it comes to how closely you follow your plan. If you stick closely to your plan and your initial steps go well, you will want to use the same approaches throughout the process. In essence, this is creating a template to follow each time you complete the chosen task. Being consistent in how you proceed with each step will help to make the whole process more systematic and keep things moving smoothly.

I mentioned earlier that most people have difficulty with consistency. This shortfall can be attributed to a number of factors. When you begin a task that you have never done before, you may sometimes miss small details of the process or procedure. Once this error occurs, it is difficult to repeat the process, because you cannot remember exactly what you did or how you did it. This doesn't mean you are suffering from early Alzheimer's; it just means you need to focus on each step and develop a keen attention to detail. Keeping a journal, notes, or other form of documentation can assist in this part of the plan, especially for those of us with bad short-term memory.

Another reason we have a hard time being consistent is that we sometimes change parts of the process as we go along. Again, try to be specific and to stick to the established plan. This is just an example of how all these elements are interdependent upon each other. At any rate, consistency is a critical component of practical planning. Implementing it throughout the life of your project will prevent a lot of headaches.

The fourth and last element of practical planning, *follow-through*, involves taking action as a consequence or extension of a previous action—that is, continuing something through to completion. This is probably the single most important part of this entire process because it brings us back to striving to be finishers. As stated earlier, finishers have a knack for implementing follow-through on a consistent basis (see how all these principles work together?), which ultimately makes it easier for them to achieve their goals.

I emphasize follow-through not only because it is a crucial part of gaining and maintaining focus but also because it is the one factor that can hold us back from completing tasks more than any other. How many times have you heard someone say, "One day I'll finish [insert important unfinished task here]"? The number-one reason for 90 percent of all things in life that are started and never finished is a chronic lack of follow-through. It is a

Casey "OZ" Osborne

crippling, debilitating disease that affects almost every person on the planet at some point in their lives. People always say hindsight is 20/20 when they reflect on things they could have done differently. Why procrastinate to your own detriment then justify your actions (or lack thereof) when it is totally and completely avoidable? The people that make these types of statements are capable of succeeding at any and everything they desire to achieve. Follow-through is the all-encompassing reason behind every principle written in this text, and it is the whole purpose of this book.

So after that little OCD outburst and without beating the proverbial horse to death, I would like to reiterate the importance of following through and becoming a finisher. To adopt and implement the principles I have given you, it is absolutely imperative that you keep your end goal at the forefront of your mind at all times. It is your imaginary carrot on a stick, dangling in front of you, and its importance must dwarf all unnecessary distractions in your life.

The pride and sense of accomplishment that comes from completing an important task can be compared to the feeling of seeing your children succeed at something they worked very hard at accomplishing. As a person who is committed to achieving goals, you must assign a similar level of importance to your own goals. I say "similar" because nothing should come before your family, especially before your offspring. But I use this analogy because your follow-through is just that crucial to your success. It is the one thing that will not allow you to fail and will guarantee your ability to complete whatever you decide to do.

Follow-through and the Three Ps will ensure that you stay motivated until you meet your goals. I'm not suggesting that you don't need the help, love, and support of your family and friends, but you are the center of your own wheel. Your own drive and determination to reach the finish line will ultimately push you toward your goal.

All these elements can make an insurmountable task seem like everyday work. If you do not acknowledge your limitations, they do not exist. This is textbook mind over matter, and anyone can do it.

Chapter 8

THE FREEDOM OF FLEXIBILITY

To be flexible is to be susceptible to modification or adaptation—to be adaptable. Our lives are finite and composed of paths that are not written in stone. If we do not allow for the unforeseen changes that life throws our way, we will struggle to continue our forward progression. Flexibility is the key to a successful outcome in almost any given situation. Our abilities to shift on the fly, adapt and overcome, and turn lemons into lemonade is what separates us from machines. We are born with the innate ability to make conscious decisions based on our personal wants and needs. It is important to remember to exercise this attribute when necessary. As you pursue your goals, this built-in talent is a blessing.

As we develop a plan, or road map, to achieve our goals, sometimes things don't go as planned. When we hit detours, we face a choice either to allow it to stifle us or to modify the original plan to fit the current circumstances. Instead of allowing unexpected events to slow or halt your progress, choose the latter of the two options. If you embrace the concept that there are always alternatives to what was planned, you will be freed from self-made constraints.

To avoid being locked into a particular course of action, establish several ways to get to where you want to be. This should be done in the initial planning stages of your overall goal. Being proactive instead of reactive is another way to "keep it moving," so to speak. Look beyond the here and now in an effort to avoid future pitfalls. Essentially, scout the route ahead in the interest of staying out in front of potential problems. I make it a point to try to think four steps ahead; that way, when I get thrown a curveball, I'm prepared to move to the backup plan. I realize that this doesn't apply in every situation, but if you adopt this type of forward thinking, it will come in handy.

Being flexible does more for you than just give you an exit strategy. It frees your mind to think outside the box, to be open to unorthodox methods of goal achievement. This is a quality that CEOs of major corporations pay big money for and sometimes outsource to acquire. The more options you give yourself in a given scenario, the less likely you are to feel trapped or stuck. That stuck feeling can make you doubt your potential for success and second-guess the pursuit of your end result. I call this the glass-half-empty effect, and it is based completely on individual perception. If you perceive your situation as dire, hopeless, or futile, it will be. But if you take a step back, reevaluate your circumstances, and consider positive alternatives, you can turn problems into power.

This power is derived from the learning that takes place when we allow ourselves to be flexible in your thinking process. Once we solve the issue of how to get from point A to point C by going around B, our brain stores that information for future use. Basically, we develop a new tool to employ should a similar situation arise later. Our brains are amazing supercomputers that process terabytes of data without us even trying. The problem is that we have a tendency to get in our own way by limiting ourselves to one type of thinking or one mind-set. Opening your mind to options you haven't previously considered will grant you the freedom to navigate around obstacles almost effortlessly. Obviously, it will take time to change your native thought process, but if you work at it a little every day, eventually it will become a part of who you are.

As individuals, we control the limitations placed on our minds, and as stated earlier, if you don't acknowledge any limits on what you can accomplish, those limits don't exist. I firmly believe in this and try to live by it daily. Failing to embrace your personal power can prevent you from reaching your full potential and ultimately prevent you from achieving your goals.

I am a fan of gadgets, electronics, and technology in general, and I frequently install car audio/video systems for people. Recently I had a request to install five monitors in a Dodge Charger, which I had never done before. To be honest, I was a little nervous because I had no idea exactly how to begin, much less how to complete the job correctly. But instead of communicating my doubt to the owner, I quickly said, "Yeah, I'll do it!" I had no clue how the headrest or visor screens were supposed to go in, but I had committed to it and was determined to succeed. I immediately began reading, researching other people's installs on the Internet, and going over my basic knowledge gained from previous installs.

I started the install and quickly ran into a few problems. I stopped, took a break, and devised a plan to get past the issue. When I finished (and made sure it all worked properly), I told the owner that it was my first time doing that kind of install. He responded, "I couldn't tell."

I use this example not to boast about my install skills but to point out that you can do almost anything you believe you can do if you stay flexible, have an open mind-set, and trust in your abilities. I like to think that there is nothing I cannot do if my will to succeed is greater than my fear of failure. I try to be positive about everything I set out to do and let life prove me wrong instead of adopting a defeatist attitude. There are enough haters in the world, so why hate on yourself?

I don't know if I am just fortunate or blessed, but every time I truly believe that I can do something and match that belief with the proportional amount of effort, I crush whatever is in front of me. By no means am I claiming to be superhuman, abnormally talented, or special in any way. In fact, as a young man I struggled to find my place among my peers and often felt that I didn't measure up to where I should be in life. It wasn't until I established a more positive, more focused outlook that I began to feel like I could do anything that anyone else could do if I simply tried really hard and believed I could do it.

To this day I can't tell you why or how it happened, but one day in November 2006, I woke up and decided that I was going to change the way I thought and how I approached every aspect of my life. I like to think that God allowed me to have a much-needed epiphany that put me where I needed to be and enhanced my spiritual and mental health. Thank You, God!

I know I don't have the market cornered on recognizing personal power and applying it to my everyday life. This is a trait that all people possess; it may simply be lying dormant in some of us. Wake it up! Tap into the endless supply of thoughts, ideas, and abilities tucked away in the deep recesses of your brain. Step outside your comfort zone and explore options you have never considered, and you will break free from your own personal prison. Once you allow yourself to be completely flexible in your thinking, your actions, and your perception of your own abilities, you can continue to move forward, no matter what life throws at you. The only person that can get in your way is you. Don't be that person. Acknowledge who you are and what you are capable of, believe in yourself, and keep it moving.

Chapter 9

STAYING OPEN TO SERENDIPITY

Serendipity is the unexpected arrival of something pleasant, valuable, or useful. Equally important to staying flexible is developing the ability to recognize and properly use serendipity to your advantage. Based on the definition provided, I'm sure you can see why I put these two topics together. Flexibility and serendipity go hand in hand, in terms of taking a potential showstopper and making it into a positive event. As stated by many notable philosophers, we are not defined by the mistakes or obstacles we encounter in life but by how we recover and move forward in the aftermath of such events.

As stated earlier, I do not subscribe to concepts such as destiny, luck, and fate, because I feel we should take positive measures to steer our lives in a desired direction. Serendipity is something different altogether; it is unplanned occurrences that are conducive to goal achievement. A true finisher recognizes the value of a serendipitous event and seamlessly integrates it into "the plan." Some argue that this is a classic example of divine intervention, and based on my own spiritual beliefs, I am inclined to agree. However, when I decided to write this book, I vowed to try to avoid personal biases based on religious or political views as much as possible.

Obviously, we cannot depend solely on serendipity to achieve our goals; hard work and the Three Ps are critical to success. Because focus is the cornerstone of success, it can be easy to become myopic and thus miss out on a great opportunity. To avoid this situation, it is important to balance focus with situational awareness. Understanding the events that take place in your environment will almost always work to your advantage. Successful people in various aspects of business and life understand the value of this concept and employ it regularly. Situational awareness not only assists in detecting fruitful prospects but also helps in avoiding negative factors that may hinder progress.

Keep in mind that taking advantage of serendipity is not always an individual endeavor. For those of us that are a part of a team or tend to work in groups, external ideas and information can be helpful. Ensure that those in your circle are on the lookout for opportunities that are conducive to your success and feel comfortable sharing their findings. Close friends, family members, and business associates with similar goals and team loyalty are exceptionally skilled at detecting serendipitous opportunities. Staying open to serendipity requires that the person or people involved embrace outside-the-box thinking. Tunnel vision is the enemy of serendipity and will cause you to miss out on your blessings.

Fluidity of thought and openness to unorthodox ideas and techniques from unlikely sources will be your ally. Sometimes we get so wrapped up in sticking to the plan that we reject the introduction of outside influences or suggestions. This can be a huge mistake because those who are removed from the epicenter of your operation have a wider field of view. It's like when you wear a certain fragrance and get to a point where you can no longer smell it, but others can pick it up immediately. Probably a strange analogy but the point is not to be too quick to disregard suggestions from others. This wide-angle vantage point can open your eyes and mind to opportunities that may have otherwise gone unnoticed.

This is an area where sometimes focus can be confused with closed-mindedness. In actuality, the two are completely different concepts that merely share some of the same attributes. The latter is a resistance to entertain anything beyond what one has decided is right. Focus, on the other hand, is the concentration of effort in a certain direction while simultaneously staying open to the possibility of alternatives that may yield the same results. Hence, focus leaves plenty of room for serendipity. Ultimately, the end goal is to avoid a myopic view of possible pathways to success.

Chapter 10

PRUDENT DECISION MAKING

Prudence is careful, good judgment that allows someone to avoid danger or risks. It is imperative to be careful not to allow your focus to impede the decision-making process. Obviously, attaining and maintaining focus is important, as I have chosen it as the overarching theme of this book. But my point is to emphasize the equally important task of exercising situational awareness when making decisions. Being oblivious to the events unfolding around you can be detrimental to the decision-making process in general. The goal should be to avoid a one-dimensional way of thinking that can slow your progress in life, business, relationships, etc.

Several factors should be taken into consideration when developing a decision-making plan of action. What is the intended end goal? What is the most practical way to approach a solution? Will the selected solution achieve the desired result? And will the desired result be sustainable for the foreseeable future? In one sense, this is the process of making a checklist to ensure that you are successful and do not duplicate your efforts.

Duplication of effort has long been one of my biggest pet peeves because I feel that you expend more time, money, and energy on trial-and-error scenarios than you do if you take time to research a more solid solution that you can test. It has been said that the definition of insanity is doing the same thing repeatedly and expecting different results. Well, doing things repeatedly without first applying some solid research and critical thinking is just as futile. Many a well-laid plan has met its demise because of duplication of effort without first conducting the proper research. This concept not only applies to decision making but also to other aspects of pursuing success in life. Even someone who sets out to purchase a vehicle, house, or other high-cost item will inevitably come out better if he or she conducts some solid research beforehand.

Another important aspect of the decision-making process is calculating the risk and impact associated with the proposed decision. If the risks or the potentially negative impacts of a given decision outweigh the benefits, then perhaps it should be reevaluated. Again, the elements of practical planning are essential to your success. Part of this planning is risk assessment and risk management. There is an entire career field dedicated to this one facet of decision making. In fact, large corporations frequently pay experts to come in and do assessments for them prior to making a serious decision that may impact their financial position. So it stands to reason that we as individuals should take the same care and consideration in our personal and professional lives, albeit on a slightly smaller scale.

Once a proposed decision has passed your personal gauntlet, the next step is implementation. It is imperative to ensure that you have all the key components in place prior to beginning. This could come in the form of finances, resources, people, or physical items needed to proceed. At any rate, these components should be identified and procured during your decision-making plan of action. Having these critical assets in place prior to the implementation phase will alleviate a potentially frustrating situation before it develops. From this point forward, implementation should be relatively simple and reasonably free of obstacles. This is not to say that you won't hit a snag or two, but the number of such instances will be minimized due to prior planning.

A good rule of thumb is to conduct routine progress checks as you move through the different steps of your decision making to ensure that you are staying on track with the intended outcome. This will allow you to identify any deviations and correct them before it is too late. Depending on the size or complexity of the task, taking such precautions can be the key to your success. Conversely, the potential frustration and disappointment associated with not practicing prudence can cripple your project and ultimately result in failure.

You may notice that a lot of the information in this chapter deals with avoiding unnecessary pitfalls, mistakes, and errors. This is not by coincidence but by design because it follows my theory on duplication of effort. It is meant to provide you with ways to circumvent otherwise avoidable situations. As my grandfather used to say, "I scraped my knees so you won't have to," which was an analogy I didn't fully grasp until I had children of my own. I may be using an obscure reference here, but if you've made it this far then you probably get it by now. Besides, isn't the point of a self-help book to keep you from making mistakes that someone else has already made? I think so. In fact, I believe it so deeply that I have dedicated the last few years to documenting my advice and experiences in an effort to keep you from scraping your knees unnecessarily.

A lack of careful consideration before making decisions can limit your ability to reach your goals. That's not to say that success *cannot* happen if mistakes are made, but making well-planned, well-thought-out, and well-researched decisions makes things a lot easier. And it goes without saying that the fewer needless errors you encounter the better.

One of the most important aspects of the whole decision-making process takes place at the end, once decisions have been selected, vetted, and fully implemented. Remember the last two questions of our decision-making checklist? Did the selected solution achieve the desired result? And is the desired result one that is sustainable for the foreseeable future? If the answer to both of these questions is a resounding yes then you very likely have a firm grasp on the concept of prudent decision making.

Chapter 11

MEETING YOUR OWN EXPECTATIONS

An *expectation* is a strong belief that something will happen or be the case in the future, that someone will or should achieve something. Many times in life, we find ourselves disappointed when certain situations don't turn out the way we expect them to. The level of disappointment increases when people that we put faith in do not perform in the way we anticipated they would. The sad reality is that the latter of these two situations is truly beyond our control. We absolutely cannot control the actions of others and therefore have only limited influence on whether they meet our expectations or not. The only thing we can do in this case is assess the situation, come up with a viable solution, and move forward in a positive manner. Dwelling on the disappointment is counterproductive and will not help us achieve our goal.

On the other hand, meeting your own expectations is completely within your control and can greatly impact your goal achievement. No one will ever be in your corner or have your back like you will for yourself. Self-preservation dictates that we strive to be our own biggest fan in terms of reaching our intended goals. A strong sense of self-confidence, a belief in your own abilities, and a copious amount of determination are the tools that will ensure you meet your own expectations.

One of the most important aspects of meeting your own expectations is to set realistic and achievable goals. This is where using backward planning and clearing your mental desk come into play. They lay the foundation for your success in terms of meeting your expectations.

It is during the early planning stages of goal achievement that we set ourselves up either for success or for failure. While it is very important to be ambitious and to set high standards for yourself, it is equally important to be honest with yourself about your ability to meet those standards. Pushing yourself to achieve more is always a good thing; just make sure you don't set goals that are clearly beyond your abilities, talents, or available resources. The resulting disappointment could be damaging to the positive perspective you have worked so hard to build.

Documenting your progress as you move through each step of your journey toward goal achievement is a good way to ensure that what is actually taking place aligns with what you expect to happen. This also allows you to make adjustments early on, should things get slightly (or severely) off track. If your goal or project involves a partner, employee, or team, it is also good to elicit input from them on how things are going. The opinions of professionals and subject-matter experts who are directly involved with your project are sometimes an excellent measure of how well your expectations are being met. That's because you and they are the most intimately familiar with the original intent and the current status.

Your job as project leader, program manager, or boss is to pay attention to the data gathered from these sources and implement changes as necessary in order to maintain movement in the right direction. Human capital is one of the most valuable assets in your arsenal of resources for goal achievement. Because of this, I caution you to ensure that you take care of your people as much as you possibly can. A happy worker is a productive worker; a productive worker is good for business; and when business is good, everybody wins. No CEO, CFO, or vice president of a company has ever made his or her business hugely successful alone. People are an integral part of any undertaking of moderate to large scale, and to underestimate their worth or contribution is a monumental mistake.

Another aspect of meeting your own expectations that frequently gets overlooked is being thorough. This goes beyond reading the fine print on contracts, spell-checking business e-mails, or verifying costs on an invoice. The thoroughness I'm speaking of is an all-encompassing mentality that permeates every action, word, or thought that goes into what you are trying to achieve. It is absolutely critical to be intimate with your project on an almost molecular level. If you are completely in-the-know as far as what is going on and how things are being accomplished, you have direct control over whether or not you meet or even exceed your expectations.

No one has a greater impact on your overall goal achievement than you do. Some call it being anal retentive; some call it micromanagement; I call it keeping your finger on the pulse of what's happening with something in which you have invested time, energy, emotion, and possibly large amounts of money. Like I said earlier, you have to be your own biggest fan, and as such you must have a vested interest in how progress is developed, implemented, and tracked. This is my personal and professional definition of being thorough. It is not one-dimensional or limited in scope, by any means. This type of thoroughness requires a level of focus that is difficult but not impossible to achieve.

The easiest way to describe it is to compare it to the way a new mother is attentive to every single thing her newborn goes through. The end goal you are attempting to achieve is the development of your newborn baby, and as a parent you are critical to its survival, its sustainment, and ultimately its success. This analogy is not uncommon; in fact, you have probably heard businesspeople say, "This new project is my baby." At any rate, the important thing is giving your goal the devoted attention that is required to see it to fruition.

Obviously, being this dedicated to something requires a lot of effort. But keep in mind that your efforts are not in vain, because they contribute directly to your success. An investment of this magnitude should never be too much to ask of yourself if it benefits you or your team in the end. Now, you may ask, isn't that a lot of pressure to put on yourself? That depends on how much you want to succeed. No one is going to push you harder than you can push yourself. The objective is to embody the very thing that you desire the most, to view it as a lofty yet attainable goal that is well within your grasp.

The only thing that can possibly stop you from attaining that goal is you—and we already stated that you should be your own biggest fan. That means at times you will be your own coach, mascot, and cheering section, if for no other reason than the fact that you know better than anyone else what waits on the other side of all your hard work. Self-motivation is the best motivation because it is free, so it has a wonderful return on investment.

If I had to summarize this chapter in a way that transcends all cultural, social, and economic barriers, I would simply say this: Decide what you expect from yourself, develop a plan to get there, focus all energy in that direction, and absolutely do not stop until you have met your expectations. We are limited only by the limitations we acknowledge, so follow this formula, and you cannot fail at your chosen task, whatever it may be.

Chapter 12

CLOSING THE LOOP

Everything we have covered up to this point has placed you in a position to be successful at whatever you choose to tackle, whether it be in life, business, school, work, or anything else of importance to you. *Closing the loop* refers to bringing things to an end or completing a series of events. This can mean adjourning a meeting, summarizing your thoughts, or finishing a specific job or task. In the case of this text, all the above can and may apply which is why I chose this as the title for the last chapter.

In this book, I have identified several concepts that are designed to provide you with a blueprint to shape and mold yourself into a confident, competent person who understands the meaning and value of focus. However, blueprints, schematics, maps, and any other forms of guidance are useless if you do not comprehend how to apply the information provided. The Law of Recency states that all things being equal, the things learned last will be best remembered. The opposite is also true: the longer a person is away from a new fact or understanding, the harder it is to remember.

To compensate for this, it is imperative to repeat and emphasize the objectives in this book that hold the most importance. So, in an attempt to close the loop, I will highlight aspects of this book that are key to your success and the success of those within your circle. The method of delivery I have chosen is basically a recap of each chapter and the points contained within each that I feel will strike a chord with you.

In chapter 1, *focus* was defined as the ability to concentrate your attention in a positive direction without straying from the intended path. I pointed out that failure to achieve a specific goal or complete a particular task can usually be attributed directly to the lack of, loss of, or inability to focus on the goal or task at hand. Chapter 1 also introduced the Three Ps, which are patience, persistence, and perseverance. These three attributes are generally what fuel us to become finishers.

Chapter 2 warns about the pitfalls of controlled and uncontrolled distractions. Managing these aspects of our lives decreases stress and increases our critical thinking abilities, thereby enhancing our focus. Chapter 3 focused on identifying and managing exposure to the people, places, and things in our lives that are subcategories of the two types of distractions mentioned in chapter 2.

Chapter 4 speaks of the importance of simplicity and of avoiding unnecessary complications in the pursuit of our goals. Chapter 5 discusses the process of identifying your goals. I also mention the concepts of clearing your mental desk, creating a road map, and lockstepping yourself through the necessary processes. Chapter 6 concentrates on the extremely important task of recognizing your own potential. I also state that it is crucial to be able to identify what you are good at and to capitalize on the qualities that will aid in your success.

Chapter 7 identifies the elements of practical planning: specificity, accuracy, consistency, and follow-through. I would like to call your attention to the fourth element in this series: follow-through. Again, the number-one reason for 90 percent of all things that are started and never finished is a chronic lack of follow-through. I repeated it because it is probably the single most important thing you should take away from this entire text. If you focus your attention on one particular aspect of what you have read, please let this be it. You may notice that some of the concepts in one chapter echo or mirror concepts in another chapter. This is done intentionally because it is congruent with the Law of Recency.

Moving on to chapter 8, we delve into the freedom of flexibility. As previously stated, "Once you allow yourself to be completely flexible in your thinking, your actions, and your perception of your own abilities, you can continue to move forward, no matter what life throws at you." Chapter 9 speaks about serendipity, which is the accidental discovery of something pleasant, valuable, or useful. A true finisher recognizes the value of a serendipitous event and seamlessly integrates it into a plan.

Chapter 10 focused on prudent decision making, and although there is plenty of useful information contained in the chapter, it can most effectively be summarized by one statement: "If the risks or the potentially negative impacts of a given decision outweigh the benefits, then perhaps it should be reevaluated." Chapter 11 deals with meeting your own expectations and is basically a reminder for us to hold ourselves accountable for the completion of the endeavors we embark on. Meeting your expectations is completely within your span of control and can greatly impact your goal achievement.

The synopsis that I have provided you with is just a small taste of the veritable cornucopia of information that you have previously consumed lol. I have no doubt that you will find yourself going back and reading all of this again if not several times. Honestly, I hope you read this book over and over again until these concepts and ideas become a part of your normal way of functioning as you seek to achieve your goals.

I took my time writing this book because I wanted to choose my words carefully and to give it and you the attention you deserve. If what I have shared helps you and anyone within your circle become a finisher and achieve what they need or desire to achieve then I have succeeded at my intended goal.

As I stated in the preface, there are hundreds and maybe even thousands of people out there with unlimited potential to succeed at whatever they desire to achieve. This book is just a basic point of reference to help us get back on track and keep moving forward.

On a personal note, I feel that I would be remiss if I didn't explain the basic motivation behind everything I have told you. I don't necessarily want my life to be easy, because I feel like that is unrealistic, and because I have learned to appreciate the growth that comes from adversity. I do, however, desire a life that is meaningful, that is filled with purpose, and that contributes positively to those with whom I come in contact. I feel that we were all put here to help one another, so for me to live any other way is an exercise in futility. Thank you for giving me your time and attention, and may life provide you with the success and happiness that we all deserve. V/R, OZ

ACKNOWLEDGMENTS

I would like to thank the following people for their help and inspiration in writing this book.

Jessinia Osborne
Jalyssa Martinez
Jayneece Kennedy
Jaylynn Kennedy
Cynthia Osborne
Dennis Felder
Melissa Bratcher
Lisa Lewis
Wendy Carroll
Danny Howard
Michael "Mikey" Brewer
A. P. Williams
James "Jim" Pappa
Jon "Andy" Feigum
Marcus Martinez
Matt Brauer
Justin Waltman
K. P. Marsilio
Ben Haines
Benjamin "Benny" Rodriguez
Brian Copper
Todd Smith
Rhodia Perry
Gerald Brooks
Sean Nichols

Casey "OZ" Osborne

Todd Weber
John Peloquin
Eric Kaziska
Dave Patton
Steve Swanson
Richard Bribiesca
Shelby McFadden
Adarryll Crawford
Robert "Bob" Wallace
Shaconda Mitchell
Stephanie Edland
Tim Ryan

ABOUT THE AUTHOR

Casey "OZ" Osborne manages a custom wheel and performance tire shop. He earned two associate's degrees from Park University in criminal justice and instructor technology and recently retired from the US Air Force as a formal training instructor and security forces supervisor. Osborne has four daughters and lives in Panama City, Florida.

Printed in the United States
By Bookmasters